Historical AMERICA

The Southwestern States

by
D. J. Herda

The Millbrook Press
Brookfield, Connecticut
The American Scene

Cover photos courtesy of (clockwise from top)
The Granger Collection; D.J. Herda; Art Resource.

Photographs courtesy of Library of Congress: pp. 6, 9,
17, 19, 22, 44, 49; The Granger Collection: pp. 12, 32;
Missouri Historical Society: p. 24; D.J. Herda: pp. 26,43,
54; Texas Tourist Agency: p. 34; National Archives: p. 40.

Library of Congress Cataloging-in-Publication Data

Herda, D.J., 1948–
Historical America. The southwestern states / by D.J. Herda.
p.   cm.—(The American scene)
Includes bibliographical references and index.
Summary: Examines the history of the Southwest and Hawaii, from
the earliest Indian inhabitants to life in the Old West and more
recent times.
ISBN 1-56294-123-2 (lib. bdg.)
1. Southwest, New—History—Juvenile literature.   2. California—
History—Juvenile literature.   3. Hawaii—History—Juvenile
literature. [1. Southwest, New—History.   2. California—History.
3. Hawaii—History.] I. Title. II. Series: Herda, D.J., 1948–
American scene.
F786.H44   1993
979—dc20   92-28206   CIP   AC

Published by The Millbrook Press
2 Old New Milford Road
Brookfield, CT 06804

CONTENTS

INTRODUCTION

Historical America: The Southwestern States traces the development of the southwestern United States, from the earliest Indian inhabitants through the statehood years, a span of more than four centuries. Few regions of America have been explored so early—or settled so late. The area made up of Colorado, New Mexico, Utah, Arizona, Nevada, and California has played a unique role in the history of the United States. So, too, has the South Pacific state of Hawaii, whose story will also be told in this book.

One of the least populated regions in America, the Southwest has been home to many different Native American cultures—from the Apache, Pima, Navajo, and Pueblo tribes of the Far South to the Ute, Hopi, Shoshone, Washo, Paiute, and Pomo of the North, as well as the Hawaiians of Polynesian descent in the South Pacific.

Despite early expeditions by the French and—to a much greater degree—the Spanish, very few Europeans ventured into the Southwest until well into the 1800s. One reason is that much of the region belonged to Mexico until the Treaty of Guadalupe Hidalgo gave the land to the United States in 1848. Few Mexican citizens were interested in relocating to these wide open spaces to the north. Another reason is that nature, in creating the great western barrier known as the Rocky Mountains, designed a formidable foe to the westward movement of Americans.

Yet not even the tallest of barriers could prevent a few hardy adventurers from struggling to discover a route to California and the West. Such intrepid men as Kit Carson, Jim Bridger, Jedediah Smith, Zebulon Pike, Stephen H. Long, and William Becknell spent years of their lives searching for the few routes westward still in use today. This same pioneering spirit lives on in much of the Southwest, where the people tend to be rugged, free-spirited, and proudly independent.

CHAPTER ONE

THE INDIANS OF THE SOUTHWEST

By the time Columbus landed in the New World in 1492, hundreds of Indian tribes were scattered throughout North America. Scholars have divided these various tribes into six main cultural areas. The northern fishermen lived in the present-day northwestern coastal states of Washington and Oregon. The Plains hunters lived in a wide band that stretched from the present-day states of Idaho, Montana, and North Dakota in the north to Texas and parts of Louisiana in the south. The Eastern Woodland Indians occupied nearly half of present-day North America from the Mississippi River valley in the west to the Atlantic Ocean in the east.

The remaining groups of Indians lived in the continental southwestern United States. These three groups included the seed gatherers, the village dwellers, and the nomads.

SEED GATHERERS

A large number of tribes lived on the high and dry plains of present-day Utah, in the hot and sandy deserts of Nevada, and among the rolling hills of California. Although much of California today is covered with lush greenery, back then it was mostly barren and brown. The area was too dry even to support corn. It would be years before white settlers would enter the region and begin digging irrigation ditches that would allow them to plant various food crops.

Despite this hostile environment, the Paiute and Western Shoshone of Nevada, the Pomo and several other tribes of central California managed to live quite comfortably in the region. Even the Ute of Colorado and Utah (after which the present-

(opposite page)
Native Americans are often pictured straddling their ponies with commanding ease. And yet Indians were not introduced to horses until the Spanish brought them to the frontier in the late 1600s.

day state is named) and the Comanche of Texas (an offshoot of the Shoshone) lived in this barren country for a time.

These Indians could not survive in the area by hunting alone, as the Plains Indians did farther to the east, for there was little game here. Nor could they survive simply by farming, as the Indians of the Eastern Woodlands did, for there was far too little rain to support the growth of food crops. Instead, they resorted to fishing and trapping wild ducks and mud hens from the area's scattered lakes and rivers. They also gathered wild nuts and seeds. The Pomo and Maidu, in fact, practically lived on acorns. They pounded them into flour, which they then washed with water to remove the bitter taste. Then they baked the soggy flour into a crude type of bread.

The Paiute and Shoshone gathered the sweet nuts that grew on dwarf pines called piñons. Other tribes gathered seeds from wild plants such as primrose and pigweed.

Most of the seed-gathering tribes traveled around the countryside, gathering each type of seed as it ripened. Each tribal family would visit from two to three different areas of the Southwest each year in their regular search for food.

VILLAGE DWELLERS

The southernmost region consisting of present-day Arizona and neighboring New Mexico was also made up mostly of dry, barren desert, although the landscape offered some relief in a few fertile green valleys, usually located along running rivers. This region had something that much of the rest of the region lacked—summer rains. The rains allowed corn and other food crops to be grown there.

Villages, called pueblos, grew up quickly in the green valleys. Some of these villages exist even today. They are occupied by tribes such as the Zuni, Hopi, Keresan, and Tanos. From their earliest existence, these tribes have led peaceful lives as farmers.

Since the village, or pueblo, dwellers had few trees or animal skins from which to build their houses, they used the desert earth and rocks. They created large terraced houses four and five stories high. Sometimes they dug caves into the steep hillsides and mountains and lived inside them. They carved

small footholds into the hillsides for climbing to the upper caves.

Besides their food crops, the village dwellers raised cotton from which they wove their clothing—breechcloths and blankets for the men and dresses for the women. Later, when the Spanish brought sheep to the area, these Indians were among the first in North America to learn to weave garments out of wool. They colored the yarn with dyes made from wild plants.

Other village-dwelling tribes, such as the Papago, Pima, Mohave, and Yuma, lived as far south as the Gila River in Arizona. Many lived in dome-shaped houses made of poles and covered with brush and earth, similar in appearance to the houses of many of the seed-gathering tribes to the north. The village dwellers, too, were primarily peaceful tribes.

Many southwestern Indians were peaceful farmers who lived in cliff dwellings called pueblos. This one, the Mesa Verde in Colorado, was discovered in 1888.

9

NOMADS

Unlike the seed gatherers and village dwellers, several tribes of Indians wandered throughout the Southwest. These were the nomads—mostly the Navajo and Apache. Originally farming tribes from Canada and Alaska, some members of these tribes eventually moved to the south and west and began wandering the area in search of food. In time, the Navajo came across the pueblo-dwelling Indians and learned from them how to grow corn and weave cotton. From the Spanish, who began exploring the region in the 1500s, the Navajos learned how to raise sheep. They followed their grazing flocks from one rich valley to another.

By the late 1600s, the nature of the Indians of the Southwest was changing. The Comanche were among the first to encounter Spanish settlers in Mexico and in what is today southern Texas. They began staging raids on Spanish settlements to obtain horses and mules. During these raids, they often captured Spanish women and children and killed the men, whom they viewed as a threat to their own lands to the north. The Pueblo Indians of New Mexico likewise obtained horses during an uprising against the Spanish in 1680.

Through skillful trading and outright theft, other tribes soon acquired breeding stock of Spanish horses, and soon use of the horse had spread throughout the tribes of the Southwest and the central Plains. Tribes that had once been farmers or nomads suddenly began flooding the Plains in search of new sources of food—most often the American bison. By the mid-1700s, these tribes included the Kiowa and Shoshone, who occupied much of the Plains region east of the Rocky Mountains; the Comanche to their south; and, during the next century, the Kiowa, who had shifted to an area between present-day Denver, Colorado, and Amarillo, Texas.

In response to the rapid spread of the Kiowa, the Comanche eventually moved south and east of Amarillo, while the Shoshone stayed to the north. These three tribes had long been close friends and allies and together controlled most of the area east of the Rockies from Montana in the north and as far south as northern Mexico.

From time to time, several northern Plains tribes staged

raids on the millions of head of bison in eastern Colorado and New Mexico. The Kiowa, Comanche, and Shoshone of the Southwest numbered nearly ten thousand. All were excellent horsemen. With the mountains at their back, they were more than a match for the invaders from the north.

OTHER SOUTHWESTERN TRIBES

Most of the other Indian tribes throughout the Southwest were much more peaceful than the Comanche. Some had survived in the region for many thousands of years.

The Anasazi of the Colorado Plateau moved to present-day Utah more than two thousand years ago. Most of the Pueblo tribes were descendants of the Anasazi. The Pueblo's cliff dwellings can still be seen in the southeastern part of the state.

As early as A.D. 800, the ancient Indians of southwestern Colorado, whose colonies dated back more than 20,000 years, had been replaced mostly by the Pueblo and several other cliff-dwelling tribes. The Ute, Paiute, Gosiute, and Navajo tribes were also living in the region by the time the first Spanish settlers arrived in the 1500s.

Only a few widely scattered tribes lived in present-day California by the time the first Europeans arrived during the early sixteenth century. These included the Hupa, Pomo, Wiyot, and Yuki in the north; the Costanoan, Miwok, and Yokuts in the central; the Mono and Koso in the east; and the Chumash, Salinan, Serrano, and Diegueño in the south.

For more than a century, these and the other Indian tribes in the Southwest had been successful in discouraging the Spaniards from moving north out of Mexico into the present-day southwestern United States. But their early successes were to be short-lived. In time, the Spaniards' superior forces and use of firearms would take their toll, and thousands of years of Native American cultures in the Southwest would be almost completely destroyed.

ata Outina.

.13.

A CLASH
OF CULTURES

By the early 1500s, the province of New Spain was a sprawling empire that included the land that is now Mexico, as well as most of the southern and western parts of the present United States. The region stretched from Florida in the east to California in the west, from the Rio Grande in the north to the Rio de la Plata in the south.

The conquistadors, or conquerors, of New Spain had been taking everything of value they could find from the area's Indian villages for years. When tales of great cities of gold throughout the American Southwest reached the capital of New Spain in present-day Mexico City, the stories fired the imagination of Spanish explorers.

In 1527, the viceroy, or ruler, of New Spain formed an expedition. A group of conquistadors was sent to explore the western coast of Florida. On its return voyage across the Gulf of Mexico, the expedition was caught in a violent storm, and the Spaniards' ship was wrecked on the reefs off the coast of Texas.

For the next six years, the survivors of the shipwreck wandered through the hot, barren deserts of Texas and northern Mexico. When the group finally found its way back to a Spanish outpost in western Mexico, only four members of the original party were left. One of the four was a Spaniard named Alvar Núñez Cabeza de Vaca. Another was an African slave named Estéban.

De Vaca told his countrymen in Mexico about the amazing land that lay just to the north. There he had seen huge humpbacked cows with curly, shaggy hair—American bison. More remarkable still, he said, were the tales he had heard of cities of great wealth that lay just a short distance north in Indian territory.

(opposite page)
This 1591 engraving shows the complex interplay of hostilities in the New World. In their search for gold, the Spanish fought countless battles, from Florida all along their westward route into New Mexico.

Cabeza de Vaca's story impressed the viceroy of New Spain. After all, according to an ancient Spanish legend, early bishops of the Catholic Church had left Spain and sailed across the Atlantic Ocean years before. They landed somewhere in the New World, where they were rumored to have built the Seven Cities of Gold before they themselves disappeared mysteriously. The cities were called Cíbola, and they were rich beyond anyone's wildest dreams. Could the stories that the Indians told de Vaca be true? And, if so, did the Indians actually know where to find Cíbola?

THE SEARCH FOR CÍBOLA

In 1539 the Spanish government sent a small group of explorers to scout the area about which de Vaca had been told. Among the explorers were Friar Marcos de Niza, a Catholic priest, and Estéban Estevanico, Marcos's guide. Estéban was the most logical person to lead the expedition. He had traveled the area before, and he spoke several Indian languages.

As the weeks turned into months, Estéban decided that the expedition would make better time if he went on ahead. He would leave markers along the way for Friar Marcos to follow.

For a while, everything went as planned. But on reaching a small Zuni Indian village, Estéban was captured and killed by angry natives.

When Friar Marcos reached the village, he learned of Estéban's fate. Marcos turned around at once and backtracked to New Spain. There he told of Estéban's murder. Then, for some reason, he went on to describe the town where the slave had been killed as larger even than Mexico City. The doorways of the stone houses, he said, were lined with emeralds, turquoise, and other precious stones. And even richer treasures lay beyond. Surely, he insisted, he had found the Seven Cities of Gold!

The Spanish could barely wait to send out another expedition. Early in 1540, Francisco Coronado set out with an army of three hundred soldiers. Four months later, he arrived at the town Friar Marcos had described. Imagine his surprise when he found not the Seven Cities of Gold but one tiny village built of earth and clay!

Coronado was stunned. Where had the gold gone? He summoned an Indian prisoner whom his troops had taken hostage and asked him about the Seven Cities. The Indian realized that his only hope for survival was to trick the Spaniards into thinking that the Seven Cities of Gold actually existed.

Yes, he told Coronado. There was a land to the east where a river six miles wide was filled with fish bigger than horses. In this land were great rulers who possessed mountains of gold. The name of this land was Quivira.

Coronado was convinced. In 1541 he set out to find Quivira. The following spring, summer, and fall, his army tramped through what is now New Mexico, Texas, Oklahoma, and Kansas. Although he never found Quivira, he believed to his dying day that the land really existed—somewhere.

THE SPANISH SETTLE CALIFORNIA

For the next two hundred years, the Spanish contented themselves with settling the lush, mountainous lands of New Spain, with only occasional journeys north. In 1769 they built the settlement of San Diego in present-day California. The settlement included a Spanish fort and a Catholic mission. Within the mission walls, Spanish priest Father Junípero Serra taught the local Indians about Christianity. He also showed them how to grow grapes, oranges, and other crops common in Europe.

During the next fifty years, the Spanish built several more forts and missions along the California coastline. These settlements stretched all the way from San Diego in the south to San Francisco in the north. The missions attracted even more Spanish settlers to the region. Many of these settlers brought cattle and started ranches beneath the warm California sun.

THE OPENING OF THE SOUTHWEST

But the Spanish soon encountered problems with several local Indian tribes. Among the most warlike was the Apache, which was actually made up of five separate groups, all closely related by language.

The Apache were kin to the Navajo and were probably originally farmers, most likely in the mountains as far south as northern Mexico. But as other Indian tribes moved into the region, the Apache turned nomadic and began raiding neighboring villages. Since they were constantly on the move, some Apache tribes began building their houses of brush, like the seed gatherers. Others made tepees, like the Plains Indians, that could be taken down and transported easily from one area to another. Most dressed in animal skins and rode horses originally descended from Spanish herds.

As a growing number of settlers began moving north, the Apache increased their raids in search of horses, firearms, and an occasional white scalp. By the early 1800s the Apache had become such a fiercely feared tribe that Spanish settlers in Mexico offered a bounty for any Apache scalps brought in. The Apache, of course, retaliated by taking even more Spanish scalps, and soon open warfare broke out throughout the land. For years, the Apache wars discouraged Spanish exploration and held Spanish settlements in the region to a minimum.

UNITED STATES GAINS A FOOTHOLD

While the Spanish in New Spain were busy fighting the Apache to the north, the United States—barely twenty years old—was growing increasingly interested in the land that lay west of Kansas, Oklahoma, and Texas. In 1803 the United States signed a treaty authorizing the purchase of the Louisiana Territory from France. The purchase nearly doubled the land holdings of the young nation. Suddenly the United States stretched as far west as central Colorado.

But the exact boundaries of the Louisiana Territory were still in question. The French, who had acquired the land from Spain, had never actually surveyed the region. At the time of the U.S. purchase, the Americans asked about the limits of the Louisiana Territory. Talleyrand, the French foreign minister who oversaw the deal, replied, "You have made a noble bargain and I presume you will make the best of it."

Indeed the Americans did. President Thomas Jefferson sent several groups of explorers into this vast new region. One of them, an army lieutenant named Zebulon Montgomery Pike, led an expedition into Colorado in 1806. Pike discovered the mountain peak that would be named for him, but he failed in

several attempts to climb it. Other American explorers, such as Stephen H. Long, also crisscrossed the region, drawing maps and making notes of what they found along the way.

It wasn't until 1818 that the United States reached an agreement with Great Britain—who claimed the region north of the Louisiana Territory—outlining the northern boundary of Louisiana. The following year, John Quincy Adams, the American secretary of state, negotiated a treaty with Spain delineating the southern and western boundaries of the territory. Everything to the north and east of that boundary was American; everything to the south and west belonged to Spain. But no one during any of these negotiations bothered to consult the primary residents of the area—the Native Americans who had lived there for centuries.

To make matters even more confusing, in 1821, Spain—

President Thomas Jefferson sent several expeditions into the newly acquired Louisiana Territory in 1805 and 1806. Zebulon Montgomery Pike became a national hero when he led a group in search of the headwaters of the Arkansas River and explored the Southwest.

which had been engaged in a bitter war with Mexico—finally granted Mexico its independence. As a result, all of Spain's land holdings in North America were turned over to Mexico. The Mexican government quickly began granting large parcels of California land to wealthy Mexican families. These families started more ranches to further strengthen Mexico's claim in the region.

That same year, a group of American horse traders led by William Becknell headed toward what they believed was still Spanish-held Santa Fe in New Mexico. Along the way, they met a group of Mexican soldiers who told them that Mexico had recently won its independence from Spain and that the Americans were trespassing on Mexican land. But once Becknell convinced the soldiers that he had come in peace to trade American goods for gold, the soldiers welcomed him. Indeed, upon his return to Missouri the following year, Becknell was reported to have emptied large sacks of silver dollars on the streets, spreading word that the Mexicans in the Southwest were eager for American trade.[1]

Becknell quickly organized a second expedition west. This time he followed a different route along the Cimarron River. Word of the new route soon spread, and before long, merchants were gathering each year at Independence, Missouri, for the long journey west along what came to be known as the Santa Fe Trail.

The Santa Fe Trail proved important to the development of the American Southwest for two reasons. It provided a route over which heavy wagons could cross the plains and the mountainous region north of Santa Fe. More importantly, it showed the Americans just how few Mexicans—including soldiers—there were in the region.

Eventually, some of the American traders who made the journey along the Santa Fe Trail decided to remain in Santa Fe. Others settled in nearby Taos, New Mexico. From their southwestern bases, they gradually began roaming still farther north and west—into present-day Colorado, Utah, and Arizona—in search of gold, silver, and furs.

But the Americans, like the Spanish before them, soon found themselves in growing conflict with the Indians. Among the most fearsome of all were the Comanche.

The Comanche had been raiding Spanish villages in search of horses and arms for decades. After Mexico had won its independence from Spain, the Comanche eased up on their raids. But when Mexican authorities began inviting American settlers to move into Mexican-held Texas, relations with the Indians once again became strained. The Comanche had experienced firsthand the determination of the Americans to build settlements on Indian land.

By the mid-1820s the Comanche and their Kiowa allies went on a rampage, attacking Americans in Texas, New Mexico, and Colorado. They burned the settlers' buildings, took their scalps, and stole their horses. The Americans retaliated by flooding the region with soldiers, building new forts to protect the settlers, and sending out well-armed military expeditions to try to force the Comanche out of the region once and for all.

William Becknell blazed the Santa Fe Trail in 1821. It remained the main trade route through the Southwest until 1880, when the Santa Fe Railroad relegated the horse and wagon to history.

THE WAR WITH MEXICO

Around 1830 the U.S. government negotiated a treaty with the Comanche. The treaty called for peace between the United States and the Indians. But at the same time, the federal government was secretly encouraging the Indians to continue their raids into Texas, which had previously declared its independence but was still claimed by Mexico.

Relations between the United States and Mexico reached an all-time low when the Mexican government refused to negotiate with American diplomat John Slidell. Slidell had been sent by President James Polk in November 1845 to negotiate the question of Texas's future, as well as to seek damages claimed by U.S. citizens living in Mexico and to attempt to purchase the Mexican-held provinces of California and New Mexico.

To make matters worse, the U.S. Congress voted to annex Texas to the United States on December 29, 1845, making it the country's 28th state. Congress then sent American troops led by General Zachary Taylor to the mouth of the Rio Grande, the river Texas claimed as its southern boundary. Mexico considered the advance of Taylor's army an open act of aggression and responded by sending *federales*, or Mexican government troops, across the Rio Grande. This was all the excuse President Polk needed to declare war, which he did on May 11, 1846.

Nearly two years later, following the storming of Mexico City by U.S. troops in September 1847, peace was reestablished by the Treaty of Guadalupe Hidalgo, signed on February 2, 1848. The treaty gave the United States most of Mexico's land holdings from Texas to California. In return, Mexico received $15 million. Five years later, the United States and Mexico signed the Gadsden Purchase, which included the purchase for $10 million of the last remaining Mexican land north of Texas's Rio Grande River.

THE LAST OF THE COMANCHE

Meanwhile, the Comanche, who had for the most part managed to live up to the terms of their peace treaty with the United States, could not understand how land could change ownership from one government to another. No person, no nation could own land, they insisted. It belonged only to the Great Spirit in the Sky, who allowed his children to use it. So the Comanche, who had for years staged raids into both Texas and neighboring New Mexico, resumed their attacks. This time, though, the raids were directed at the Americans.

Comanche war parties proved such a stubborn foe that the United States government was finally forced to send a large number of troops into the area. Government officials met with Comanche and Kiowa chiefs and convinced the leaders of the two tribes that, unless they lay down their arms and surrendered, the full force of the "white knives," as the Indians called them, would be thrown against them. The tribes reluctantly agreed to terms, signed a peace treaty, and moved to separate reservations in Oklahoma.

THE SETTLING OF CALIFORNIA

After Mexico had won its independence from Spain in 1821, California (then known as Alta California) had become part of the new Mexican nation. During the 1840s, Mexico began selling many of its government missions to private individuals. Thousands of large California estates were started in this way.

By the late 1840s, a few hundred U.S. citizens had moved into Mexican-owned California to farm, hunt, and trade with the Mexican landowners. One of these Americans was John A. Sutter, a Swiss immigrant who owned a large parcel of land near present-day Sacramento. Sutter's land would eventually change the course of Californian—and American—history with the discovery of gold.

In 1845 another American adventurer, Captain John C. Frémont, a young captain in the U.S. Army Topographical Corps, led a government mapping expedition into California. Frémont arrived at John Sutter's fort on the Sacramento River in December. From there, he traveled to Monterey, where he was met and questioned by Mexican officials. Frémont insisted that his visit was friendly and purely exploratory, but the arms and equipment of his men aroused the suspicions of the Mexicans. When Frémont left Monterey and traveled south instead of north, the suspicions grew stronger.

General José Castro, the Mexican commander at Monterey,

sent word that Frémont and his men must leave California. Instead, Frémont began building a crude fort on Gabilan Peak, twenty-five miles northeast of Monterey. There, he planted a young tree in the ground and raised the American flag in defiance of the Mexican government. Frémont had decided that California should belong to the United States, and he was prepared to do whatever was necessary to see his dream come true.

Three days later, a Mexican force including cavalry and artillery units began to gather in the valley below Frémont's fort. Later that day, when the American flagstaff toppled in the wind and fell to the ground, Frémont took it as a bad sign. Under cover of darkness, he and his men withdrew north toward Oregon.

Although Frémont had failed in his attempt to take control of California from Mexico, word soon spread of his exploit. In 1846, as the war with Mexico broke out, he moved back south to Sacramento and began encouraging the Americans he met there to rebel against Mexican rule. Many American Californians—some settlers, others reckless adventurers— were determined to join Frémont in whatever pro-American venture he had in mind.

This 1871 lithograph shows different ways of mining for gold. In the foreground, men are sluicing gold flakes from a creek bed, while behind them, men dig the glittering substance from the ground.

Finally, on June 14, 1846, a party of thirty-three Americans attacked the northern Mexican outpost at Sonoma. Mexican officials and civilians were arrested and a makeshift flag of independence was raised. The flag had a single star, a grizzly bear, and the words "California Republic" on it.

The settlers gave up their dream of independence for California only after learning that the United States and Mexico had gone to war. Frémont's adventure came to be called the Bear Flag Revolt.

Finally, on July 7, 1846, Commodore John D. Sloat claimed California for the United States by raising the U.S. flag over Monterey. California was officially transferred to the United States some two years later under the treaty that ended the war with Mexico in February 1848.

GOLD!

On January 24, 1848, a few days before the signing of the Treaty of Guadalupe Hidalgo, prospectors discovered gold near a sawmill owned by John Sutter on the South Fork of the American River. Word of the strike traveled quickly, and by December 5, gold fever had spread throughout the world. More than 80,000 people swarmed to California during 1849 alone. The Mexicans who had been living there soon became the minority as the promise of fast wealth brought thousands of "Forty-niners" (as those who rushed to California in 1849 were called) eager to stake their claims. Other people poured in from Canada, Australia, Hawaii, England, Ireland, China, and France.

From 1848 to 1850, California's population more than tripled, reaching 93,000 people—more than enough to qualify it for statehood. But one problem remained. The U.S. Congress was deeply embroiled in the question of slavery. Northern political leaders, who were anti-slavery, wanted California admitted as a "free" state in which slavery was prohibited. Southern leaders, on the other hand, wanted to extend their influence in Congress by having California admitted as a "slave" state in which slavery was allowed. Finally, on September 9, 1850, after weeks of heated debate, California was admitted to the Union as a free state, the country's 31st.

EAST MEETS WEST

By the mid-1800s, settlers from Texas, Oklahoma, and Kansas had begun moving west into New Mexico and Colorado. The number of settlers who made the journey from the East remained small, mostly because of tales they had heard of the "Great American Desert." Most easterners were convinced that Colorado—and most of the Southwest, for that matter—was unsuitable for human settlement.

One group of easterners who failed to share those beliefs was the Mormons, a New York religious sect founded by Joseph Smith. The Mormons had their own unique beliefs about Christianity and the Bible. The sect eventually angered its neighbors and was forced to move from New York to Kirtland, Ohio, then to several sites in Missouri, and finally in 1839 to Nauvoo, Illinois. There they lived in relative peace for five years until Smith was arrested and jailed in Carthage, Illinois, for his radical beliefs. An angry mob attacked the jail on June 27, 1844, and Smith and his brother were taken from their cells and shot.

Realizing that the Mormons would have to move once again for their own safety, Brigham Young, who took over leadership of the church, decided upon a location far enough away to allow the Mormons to worship as they chose. He selected a spot near the Great Salt Lake in present-day Utah. The area, according to explorer John Frémont, was guarded by mountains to the east and north, deserts to the west and south, and fed by mountain streams of melting snow.

But when the Mormons finally arrived at Salt Lake in July 1847, they found not a paradise on Earth, but rather a barren, hostile land. One member of the church wrote later that it was "a broad and barren plain hemmed in by mountains . . . the paradise of the lizard, the cricket, and the rattlesnake."[1]

(opposite page)
Leaving the Old Homestead, *by James Wilkins, who traveled in the West in 1849, shows that some pioneers came from well-to-do families.*

Nevertheless, by the end of 1848, the Mormons through hard work and dedication had begun building an irrigation system that would eventually help them turn the brown Utah desert green with vegetation.

The Mormons had barely arrived in Utah when the United States obtained the land from Mexico in 1848. Young's attempts to organize an independent Mormon state named Deseret were thwarted when Congress annexed the Territory of Utah in 1850. Still, the Mormons continued to grow and prosper under the leadership of Young, who was eventually named territorial governor.

The Mormon leader Brigham Young chose this desolate spot near the Great Salt Lake in Utah as a haven from persecution suffered by Mormons in the East.

GOLD IN COLORADO

In 1858 word of another gold strike—this one near present-day Denver—reached the Eastern Seaboard, and large numbers of Americans suddenly changed their minds about the "Great

American Desert." Perhaps the Southwest wasn't such a bad place to live after all, they thought. People by the thousands swarmed down upon the mining camps that had been thrown together at Aurora, Central City, Gold Hill, Boulder, and Cripple Creek.

But the Colorado strike proved to be far less profitable than most people had hoped. While a few prospectors grew wealthy, most failed to find enough gold to pay their expenses west.

Nevertheless, by the mid-1800s, gold fever had gripped tens of thousands of Americans, and soon prospectors began moving farther west into Utah and Nevada in search of new, more promising strikes. Around the same time, another group of miners traveled southwest into Arizona, where they discovered silver and copper near Tubac and Ajo. Americans had only recently awakened to the vast potential of rich ore strikes in Arizona, which the United States had obtained from Mexico after the Gadsden Purchase of 1853.

Throughout the period of the Civil War, from 1861 to 1865, very little fighting took place in the Southwest. Even when Confederate forces began moving into New Mexico, few people raised an eyebrow. The only major skirmish in the region occurred in March 1862, when Southern Confederate soldiers met Northern Union troops in the battle of La Glorieta Pass near Santa Fe, the Confederate-held southwestern territorial capital.

CLASH AT LA GLORIETA

Confederate major Charles L. Pyron had learned from spies of a group of Union soldiers marching on Santa Fe from Fort Union, a nearby Union army stronghold. Pyron, knowing that the fort's garrison was small, believed he could surprise and defeat the Union troops on the narrow mountain stretch of the Santa Fe Trail outside of town. What Pyron didn't realize was that a large, well-armed group of Colorado reinforcements led by Colorado-born major John M. Chivington had recently joined the Fort Union troops.

Accompanied by four hundred men and two large cannons, Pyron started eastward to meet the Union soldiers. At La

Glorieta Pass, a high, rugged section of the Santa Fe Trail that twisted through the southern tip of the towering Sangre de Cristo Mountains, the two armies clashed.

The first Union troops to meet Pyron's battalion consisted of 418 infantry and cavalry led by Chivington. Pyron, who soon discovered that this was only part of a thousand-man Union brigade, quickly withdrew his men across a wooden bridge spanning a fifteen-foot gorge, then destroyed the bridge behind them. But that didn't stop Chivington, who, "with a pistol in each hand and one or two under his arms," according to historian Ovando Hollister, urged his troops forward.

Under heavy Confederate fire, the Coloradans charged down the narrow road leading to the gorge, then urged their horses to leap across, yelling as they headed for the rebel position. The frantic charge, according to one Texas rebel who later wrote his wife, looked like "so many flying devils" and completely stunned the Confederates. ". . . nothing like lead or iron seemed to stop them, for we were pouring it into them from every side like hail in a storm. In a moment these devils had run the gauntlet for a half mile, and were fighting hand to hand . . . in the road."[2]

Over the course of the next few days, several more battles— each nearly as bloody and every bit as dramatic—took place throughout New Mexico. When the fighting finally ended, the Union Army was left in complete control of the region. It was the Union's most important victory in the Southwest. It was also the beginning of the end for the Confederacy's dream of conquering the region.

Chivington and his men at La Glorieta Pass had fought the full force of Confederate soldiers and won. The victory became known as "The Gettysburg of the West."[3]

THE LAST GREAT FRONTIER

Meanwhile, the Civil War was unfolding in quite a different manner in nearby Nevada Territory. From the start, the region had remained solidly under control of Union forces. The discovery of large silver deposits helped to fund the Union's participation in the war. Partly in appreciation for its support to the

Union cause and partly in an effort to prevent the Confederacy from gaining control of the region's wealth, Congress admitted Nevada to the Union on October 31, 1864. The state was nicknamed, aptly enough, the Silver State.

By the time the Civil War had ended, the American Southwest consisted of only two states—California and Nevada. The other present-day southwestern states were still territories. But California and Nevada were important both to the country's economy and to the idea that America now extended from Atlantic to Pacific—"from sea to shining sea." Soon, travelers to California and Nevada would open up new avenues of travel for other American settlers, who were beginning to discover the allure of the American Southwest.

But the opening of the Southwest to settlement took place slowly. The region was still America's last great frontier. There were no people crammed shoulder-to-shoulder into sprawling cities like there were back East. What difference did it make to a man carving his way through the high mountain passes of Colorado or Utah whether or not the southwestern territories were ever settled? Throughout the Southwest, people were more concerned with survival than with questions of states and territories.

THE SEARCH FOR GOLD

Like most other westerners, Pete O'Reilly and Pat McLaughlin gave little thought to the settlement of the Southwest. Instead, they wondered how long it would be before they grew rich. O'Reilly and McLaughlin were recent Irish immigrants who had gone west to search for gold. When they heard that a prospector had struck gold near Pike's Peak, Colorado, they hurried to cash in on the good fortune. But like most other prospectors who went west to find gold, O'Reilly and McLaughlin came up empty-handed.

Dejected but determined, the two fortune hunters moved farther west to the Sierra Nevada Mountains in present-day Nevada. There, at Six Mile Canyon, they met a man named Henry Comstock who talked the immigrants into taking him in as a partner.

Before long, O'Reilly and McLaughlin discovered a rich seam of blue-colored rocks. They had never seen such rocks before, so they took a sample to town to show to a couple of wealthy Californians. The Californians realized that the rock was filled with silver, but they didn't tell that to the prospectors. Instead, they said the rock was virtually worthless.

As the evening passed, the Californians offered to buy the claim for a few hundred dollars. Comstock, who considered himself a shrewd businessman, persuaded the Californians to raise their offer to two thousand—a small fortune in the 1800s. The Californians finally agreed, and Comstock quickly set about town, boasting of how he had gotten the best of the two greenhorns from California.

Within days, the new owners of the mine began bringing men and equipment to the site. In a matter of weeks, they were extracting huge quantities of rich silver ore from the mine. Over the next twenty years, the piece of land that Comstock had sold for $2 thousand had produced more than $300 million worth of silver! The rich vein of ore from which the silver came was named the Comstock Lode.

News of the Comstock Lode spread quickly throughout the country. Before long, thousands of prospectors from every corner of the state were rushing into the area, eager to duplicate the find. A handful of them hit large strikes of their own, but much of the silver in the area was too deeply buried to dig up with picks and shovels. Only the use of large, very expensive mining equipment could unearth it. Eventually, most of the prospectors who had come to Nevada to get rich ended up working for large mining companies. But few ever gave up their hope of someday striking it rich themselves.

DESPERATELY SEEKING SILVER

The gold and subsequent silver rushes of the late 1800s lasted less than thirty years. But within that time, tens of thousands of farmers and city people, poor whites and former black slaves poured into the southwestern United States. All dreamed of striking it rich overnight, as they had heard others had done. The American Southwest was truly the land of opportunity— or at least that's what many Americans now thought.

But mining for gold and silver was a difficult, dirty, and dangerous occupation. A typical mining camp had as many as seventy-five white Americans, twenty or thirty black Americans, thirty or forty Chinese, thirty or forty Mexicans, and forty or fifty European immigrants working side by side. What it *didn't* have were laws and police. Miners were in constant danger of attack from bandits, thieves, and even other miners. Many miners lost their lives not digging for ore but fighting off those who had become so desperate for wealth that they would kill for it.

Of course, news of any large gold or silver strike spread quickly. Small towns grew into large ones in a matter of weeks as miners and merchants poured into the area to take part in the strike. Before long, a string of wooden stores would sprout along Main Street. There the miners would buy the tools, clothing, food, and supplies they needed to keep going.

Most of these mining towns boomed for only as long as the ore held out. Once the gold and silver were gone, the miners moved on. Without miners to purchase their wares, the merchants soon packed up and left. In time, the Southwest was dotted with old mining communities—called ghost towns— that had long since been abandoned.

There were some exceptions, of course. If a mining town grew large enough to support doctors, lawyers, teachers, and ranchers before the ore ran out, it might well continue to flourish even after the miners moved on. In this way, mining provided the foundation for many of the present-day towns of the Old Southwest.

CONNECTING THE CONTINENT

As the Southwest continued to grow, Congress decided that the nation needed a transcontinental railroad—a rail line connecting the country from east to west. In 1862, Congress granted two railroad companies the right to build the nation's first transcontinental railroad. It loaned money and gave free land to the Central Pacific, which began laying tracks in Sacramento, California, and to the Union Pacific, which began laying tracks in Omaha, Nebraska. The plan was to have the tracks meet somewhere midway between Sacramento and

This 1868 lithograph by Currier & Ives, Westward the Course of Empire Takes Its Way, shows the pride Americans took in their first transcontinental railroads.

Omaha, at which time the transcontinental railroad would be complete.

The railroad, as Congress envisioned, would be helpful in bringing settlers from the East to the open lands of the West. It would also bring thousands of workers to the Southwest—some of whom were bound to stay on after the railroad was complete.

Many of the people working for the Central Pacific were Chinese immigrants, while most of those working for the Union Pacific were Irish immigrants. Others included Mexican

Americans, black Americans, and American Indians. Follow- ing the Civil War, a large number of army veterans seeking employment joined the railroad work crews as well.

Working for the railroad was both difficult and dangerous. The Central Pacific workers had to lay tracks around and sometimes even through mountains. At first, their only tools were pickaxes and shovels, for dynamite had not yet been invented. By the mid-1860s, though, they began using powerful explosives, including dynamite, which was invented in 1866. While these explosives made the workers' jobs easier, it also made them far more dangerous.

As the Central Pacific workers pushed their way through the Sierra Nevada mountains toward Utah, the Chinese worked around the clock. When the crew reached a steep gorge, they would carve a roadbed for the tracks out of the side of the cliff—sometimes a thousand feet or more above the gully below. In order to blast away the rock, the Chinese were lowered down the face of the cliff in large wicker baskets. Once they reached the blasting site, they drilled holes in which to stuff the dynamite, lit the fuses, and were pulled back up the cliff as quickly as possible. Many lost their lives in the effort.

One Californian whose Chinese ancestors had worked on the railroad remembers hearing about the dangerous work from her grandfather. "You know that expression, 'a Chinaman's chance'? I always heard that it started with those men that went down the cliff in baskets."4 For all their work, the Chinese received payments ranging from twenty-six to thirty-six dollars a *month*!

Finally, on May 10, 1869, the Union and Central Pacific railroads met at a place called Promontory Point in Utah. There, railroad officials and politicians celebrated the completion of the nation's first transcontinental railroad by driving a golden spike into the last railroad tie.

Telegraph wires sent the message to a jubilant nation. The United States was officially joined from East to West. Over the next fifteen years, several other railroad companies built additional cross-country lines. By 1885 the United States had been joined by a growing network of gleaming ribbons of steel. Nothing, it seemed, could stop the country's westward expansion now.

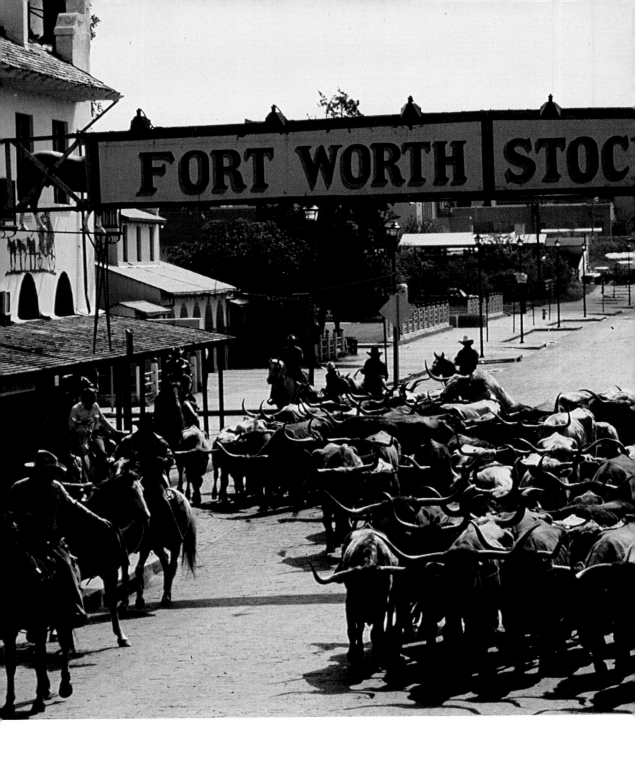

CHAPTER FOUR

LIFE ON
THE RANGE

The need for a transcontinental railroad grew not only from the desire of the American people to move west, but also from the need to move cattle to the lucrative markets of the North and East. As far back as the early 1500s, the Spanish had begun importing cattle from Spain to what is today northern Mexico and southern Texas. By the time Texas entered the Union in 1845, the state had about five million cattle. These were mostly free-roaming animals that bred freely and belonged to anyone with the courage to capture them.

Shortly before the Civil War in 1861, several Texans had begun gathering these cattle to breed on large ranches. By the time the Civil War had ended in 1865, some of these ranchers were earning huge profits from their cattle businesses.

But the ranchers soon realized that, instead of selling their cattle locally for three or four dollars a head, they could sell them for ten to twenty times as much to buyers in the East. The only problem was that the cattle needed to be shipped to market via railroad, and the closest railroad to Texas was in Missouri, several hundred miles away. Then one of the ranchers had an idea. If they couldn't bring the railroad to the cattle, they would have to bring the cattle to the railroad.

In 1866 the ranchers brought their cattle together in one large herd. They hired a few dozen men on horseback to oversee the journey. These men included Mexican *vaqueros*, or cowboys, and a number of former Civil War cavalrymen who eventually came to be called cowboys.

Over the next three months, the cowboys moved thousands of cattle from Texas to the railhead in Sedalia, Missouri. The drive—the first of many to be held each spring—was long,

(opposite page)
The past comes alive as the hooves of longhorn cattle resound against pavement at the entrance to the Fort Worth stock-yards in Texas.

hard, and dangerous. Many cattle were lost to disease, predators, and bandits along the way. Still, enough cattle reached the
railroad in Sedalia to make their owners rich.

The next large drive was organized by Joseph G. McCoy, an
Illinois livestock dealer who realized the enormous potential
for profits from shipping cattle north to the booming city of
Chicago. McCoy chose Abilene, Kansas—to which the railroad had recently come—as his shipping point north. He built
stock pens, barns, loading chutes, and a hotel to house the
cowboys upon their arrival. In September 1867 the first ship-
ment of Texas beef arrived in Chicago. Abilene soon grew into
the greatest of the region's many cowtowns, and McCoy grew
rich.

Before long, cattle ranching spread from Texas into New
Mexico and Colorado. Wherever grass was plentiful enough for
cattle to graze on, huge ranches quickly sprouted. And the era
of the American cowboy was born.

A BREED APART

It didn't take long for the rest of America to become infatuated
with the aura surrounding the American cowboy. Newspaper
reporters from Chicago to New York regularly ran stories about
this new breed of man who lived on the open range, fought
desperate criminals and savage Indians, and sang the cattle to
sleep each night.

But the real cowboy was quite unlike the tall tales told about
him around the country. Cowboys were mostly young men—
many barely in their teens. Many were blacks who had been
freed from slavery following the Civil War. Others were Mexicans who had long ago settled in the Southwest and knew the
land well.

Although the cowboys lived a dangerous life during the
spring trail drives east, most of their time was spent riding up
and down the boundary lines of their bosses' ranches, trying to
keep their cattle from roaming onto a neighboring ranch or
getting stolen. Fences hadn't yet come to the Southwest, so
riding the range was an important part of a cowboy's daily life.

In spring, the cowboys participated in roundups. They used

their lassos to catch newborn calves, which they then wrestled to the ground and branded, or marked, with hot irons. The brands were used to prove ownership. Each ranch had a different brand for its cattle.

Once the drive to market began, cowboys worked hard at keeping their herds together. They carried guns to drive predators like coyotes and wolves away from the young and sick and to discourage cattle rustlers from riding down out of the foothills and stampeding part of the herd to sell off illegally.

For all this work, a cowboy earned about a dollar a day, which was still nearly twice as much as the average American worker. Once a herd reached its destination, the trail hands received their pay, which was often spent in a few wild days of gambling and drinking. Then the cowboys would mount their horses and head back cross-country to the ranch to begin the process all over again.

NEW INDIAN UPRISINGS

While the trail drives were unfolding between Texas and Kansas, several new Indian uprisings were taking place to the north and west. As white settlers continued pushing their way into the Southwest, a group of Colorado tribes joined together to take action.

In the spring of 1864, several war parties began attacking ranches and wagon trains traveling west along the South Platte Trail. The raids reached a climax on June 11, when the Indians attacked a ranch just twenty-five miles southeast of Denver. In the brutal attack, they killed a settler, his wife, and his two daughters. Denverites responded by demanding that the U.S. government remove *all* Indians—whether peaceful or not—from the area.

Colorado governor John Evans sent word to the Arapaho and Cheyenne to return at once to their Sand Creek reservation. The Indians reluctantly agreed and returned the following fall. Peace had finally come to south central Colorado. But the U.S. army colonel stationed in the area, John M. Chivington, was not interested in peace. He wanted instead to teach the Indians a lesson they would never forget.

Chivington quietly moved his army regiment to Fort Lyon on Sand Creek, where the Indians had been promised protection. There, at sunrise on November 29, Chivington's militia attacked the Indian camp flying a white flag of truce. Shortly after the surprise attack, Chivington lost control of his men, who ended up slaughtering some 450 peaceful Indians—men, women, and children. George Bent, a half-Cheyenne who had been in the camp at the time, later described the brutal scene: "The Indians all began running, but they did not seem to know what to do or where to turn. The women and children were screaming and wailing, the men running to the lodges for their arms and shouting advice and directions to one another."

News of the massacre soon reached Washington, where the Congressional Joint Committee on the Conduct of the [Civil] War ended its investigation by condemning Chivington for having "deliberately planned and executed a foul and dastardly massacre which would have disgraced the veriest savage among those who were the victims of his cruelty."[1] General Nelson A. Miles publicly rebuked Chivington, calling the attack the "foulest and most unjustifiable crime in the annals of America."[2]

The Indians who had survived the massacre vowed revenge. They joined together in January 1865 and attacked several white settlements, including the station and stores of Old Julesburg in the northeastern corner of the territory. They returned the following month to continue their plunder and eventually burned the town to the ground.

Finally, in October 1867, Cheyenne and Arapaho leaders agreed in the Medicine Lodge Creek Treaty to move their people to a reservation in Indian Territory in present-day Oklahoma. As a result, the area of Colorado east of the Rocky Mountains was free of hostile Indians, and the whites were quick to begin constructing railroads, digging irrigation ditches, and expanding their herds of cattle northward from Texas.

Meanwhile, the Ute, who were living in the high Rocky Mountain passes of Colorado, Utah, and New Mexico, had acquired horses and begun terrorizing neighboring Indian villages. They seldom came into conflict with whites because the

Indians' range was so far removed from white settlements. Still, the U.S. government decided to remove the Ute in order to open the area to American exploration and settlement.

At first, the Ute agreed to a government offer to relocate the tribe to several remote areas in Utah, Colorado, and New Mexico. But before the move was completed, several war parties broke away and once again began attacking neighboring Navajo and Pueblo villages. Finally, in 1879, they attacked and destroyed several buildings of the U.S. Indian Agency, which had been established to keep peace between the Indians and the United States. The government sent troops to the area to end the hostilities once and for all. After a brief scuffle, the last remaining Ute surrendered and agreed to move to the reservation in Utah.

As the Comanche, Kiowa, and Ute continued to suffer the relentless pursuit of the U.S. government, other Indian tribes began filtering into the region. One of these was a large raiding party made up mostly of Apache warriors. The Apache warriors had become so numerous that Mexico and the United States jointly threatened the tribe with all-out war. This merely angered the Apache, who responded by stepping up their attacks. By the mid-1870s, Apache chief Victorio and his band of renegades were traveling up and down the territory at will. Wherever they went, they left a bloody trail of white settlers and U.S. soldiers. Victorio was finally cornered and killed in Mexico in 1880 in a battle with the *federales*.

GERONIMO JOINS THE FIGHT

After the fall of Victorio, a new Apache warrior stepped forward to take command of the tribe. His name was Geronimo, and he soon gained a reputation as the fiercest Indian leader in the Southwest.

Geronimo's raids on white settlements took up where Victorio's had left off. His warriors scoured the countryside by day, looking for likely places to attack. By night, the Indians would slip back into the protection of the rugged foothills and mountains of the Sierra Madre. For more than ten years, Geronimo's tribe managed to escape capture at the hands of the U.S. Army.

8372

Finally, in 1883, General George Crook took charge of the U.S. campaign against Geronimo. After months of pursuit, Crook finally caught and defeated the Apache chief in a vicious battle. Geronimo was forced to move onto the San Carlos reservation in Arizona. Within two years, Geronimo and most of his braves had escaped.

Before long, the Apache renewed their warfare against white settlers in Arizona and New Mexico. When word reached Washington that Crook had allowed Geronimo to escape, the general was promptly replaced by General Nelson Miles who, with several thousand troops, chased the renegade Apache across the rugged terrain of the old Southwest. Up blind canyons, across wide *arroyos*, or gullies, and through burning desert sands they roared, with the Apache out ahead and the army in hot pursuit. Finally, in 1886, Geronimo and his warriors were once again cornered and forced to surrender.

Following the capture, Geronimo was placed in a military prison in Florida before later being moved to Fort Sill, Oklahoma, where the Apache chief died in 1909. His people (including men, women, and children) were held in prison until 1913, when they were finally released and taken to a reservation in Arizona.

The defeat of the Apache ended the last of the great Indian wars in the Southwest. Now, the only thing left standing between the vast territory west of Kansas and the hoards of settlers anxious to claim it was the ruggedness of the land itself.

RANCHING CONTINUES TO SPREAD

As the railroads inched their way west from Missouri through Kansas, Texas, Colorado, and New Mexico, ranching began to spread into Arizona, Utah, Nevada, and southern California. Cowtowns sprouted in Ellsworth, Wichita, Newton, Baxter Springs, and Dodge City—all in Kansas—as well as in Ogallala, Nebraska; Cheyenne, Wyoming; and Miles City, Montana. With them came a new brand of lawlessness unknown anywhere else in the country. Bandits seeking to prey on cowboys suddenly flush with cash filled the cowtowns.

*(opposite page)
Apache chief Geronimo was one of the most fierce and tireless opponents to settlers in the Southwest. His death on February 17, 1909, signaled the end of the Apache way of life.*

41

Con men targeted the unwary. Entire gangs of rustlers—the James Brothers, the Daltons, Butch Cassidy and the Sundance Kid, and others—traveled throughout the region in their search for illegal riches.

In response, ranchers began using "hired guns"—gunmen who sold their services to the highest bidders—to keep the peace. The U.S. government, too, began sending federal marshals, including some of the most famous names in southwestern history, to such wild and remote places as Dodge City, Tombstone, and Abilene. Quick-draw experts such as Wyatt Earp, Doc Holliday, and Wild Bill Hickok (who themselves had been known to skirt the law from time to time) all served time behind a badge protecting their towns from a rapidly growing new breed of bandit.

By the early 1880s, ranching had become the single most important part of the Southwest's economy. Ranchers were busily engaged in building their herds and searching far and wide for new, lush pastures on which to graze their cattle. Herds that had once numbered a few hundred head now reached to the tens of thousands. Each new calf born in the spring represented money in the bank to its owner. Fortunes were made within a short period of time.

Then tragedy struck.

THE END OF AN ERA

By the mid-1880s, the cattle grazing the southwestern rangeland far outnumbered the market's demand for beef. Prices for cattle began to fall. Meanwhile, the growing number of cattle began placing a severe strain on the land. Once-lush grassy meadows were soon eaten clean, and the cattle had to be moved to new areas to prevent them from starving.

Then, in 1885–1886, a wicked cold winter struck the Southwest. High winds and deep snows killed off many of the cattle. The following summer offered little relief. A severe drought destroyed much of the region's grassland and dried up its streams. Still more cattle died from lack of food and water.

The following winter proved even worse than the one before. Heavy blizzards and deep snows once again blanketed much of the Southwest's high country, where most of the cattle were

grazing. The snow was so deep by mid-December that the cattle couldn't reach the grass beneath it. By the time spring came the following year, dead cattle littered the range. Within two years, nearly half of the region's cattle had died. Thousands of ranchers were financially ruined.[3]

The few ranchers who survived the disaster realized that they could no longer depend upon grazing cattle on the open range. They began fencing their cattle in and raising enough feed to see them through the harshest of winters and driest of summers. In the process, the role of the cowboy quickly changed. No longer was his a solitary life of riding the open range. Now he spent most of his time digging holes and mending broken fences. By 1890 the romance of the American cowboy had come to an end. With it ended one of the most glamorous—if fictionalized—eras in American history.

The era of the freewheeling cowboy who drove his herd on the open range has long been over, but the romance lives on.

CHAPTER FIVE

WEST TO HAWAII

The Pacific islands making up the present-day state of Hawaii developed in a much different way from the continental south-western United States. Because of Hawaii's location halfway between California and Asia, the island paradise—a few small parcels of land surrounded by hundreds of thousands of miles of water—was inhabited first by very different races of people than those who settled North America.

Hawaii is the northernmost point of the sprawling area of Pacific Ocean islands known as Polynesia. The other major island groups include New Zealand and the Easter Islands.

Historians are not sure when the first people came to the Hawaiian Islands. Some believe it was as early as A.D. 300; others think it was somewhat later. These first Hawaiians may have followed a long route through southeastern Asia, down through Indonesia, and across Melanesia before settling the Polynesian islands of Tonga and Samoa as early as 1000 B.C. From there they eventually migrated to the more distant islands of Hawaii.

Between A.D. 400 and 900, a second group of Polynesians— these from Tahiti and the Marquesas Islands—came to Hawaii. They traveled great distances across the ocean in large canoes fitted with primitive sails. The journeys of these travelers must have been long and dangerous, and many earlier expeditions were most likely lost in rough seas.

These people were joined by a new wave of Tahitians and neighboring islanders around A.D. 1000. When they reached Hawaii, they conquered the natives already living there and made them their slaves, forcing them to build temples, carve out irrigation canals, and dig ponds for fish. These conquerors were led by a great Tahitian navigator named Hawaii-loa. Together with a group of brave explorers, Loa set off on an

(opposite page)
The lush beauty of the Hawaiian landscape is captured in this painting by Jules Tavernier, a French-born artist who died in Honolulu in 1889.

expedition in giant double-hulled canoes, much like those still used by some cultures today.

The last wave of Tahitians, led by the powerful *kahuna*, or high priest, Paao, arrived in Hawaii around 1300. Soon after, the skill of making oceangoing canoes was lost, and the waves of Tahitians arriving in Hawaii stopped. The people of Hawaii became isolated from their distant island neighbors and remained so for more than a thousand years.

THE EUROPEAN INVASION

The first European to discover the islands was probably a Spanish explorer named Juan Gaetano in 1555. Other ships followed shortly thereafter. But the Spaniards kept their Pacific discoveries a secret. No written accounts of their early journeys have been found, with the exception of a few ancient maps showing the general position of the islands in the ocean.

The first European on record to reach the islands was Captain James Cook, an explorer and navigator in the British Royal Navy. On January 18, 1778, Cook spotted the islands of Oahu, Kauai, and Niihau while on a journey to search for a northern passage across North America to the Atlantic Ocean. Cook, who had previously discovered Tahiti and the Society Islands, found nothing so beautiful or enchanting as Hawaii. But strong winds and high seas kept Cook's ships, the *Discovery* and the *Resolution*, from attempting a landing that day.

The following day, with Cook's ships moored off the island of Kauai, several dozen Hawaiians sailed out in canoes to welcome the Europeans. The Hawaiians must have been puzzled by the strange-looking travelers, but they nonetheless proved eager to trade their fish and sweet potatoes for various metal objects. In his written accounts of the meeting, Cook expressed surprise at the strong similarity between the Hawaiians and the Tahitians.

After two weeks of stocking provisions aboard his ships, Cook's expedition left the islands and headed north, where they explored the coast from Oregon through the Bering Straits as far north as the Arctic Ocean. Cook returned to the islands the following November, and in January 1779 he discovered

Kealakekua Bay on the big island of Hawaii. More than a thousand canoes came out to greet him.

When Cook came ashore the next day, he was met by the high priest and taken to a temple lined with human skulls. Wherever the captain went, the Hawaiians fell to the ground in worship. They had mistaken him for the legendary god of the harvest, Lono. According to legend, Lono was to appear to the natives on a large floating island. Imagine their surprise when they saw Cook's ships with their tall masts and billowing sails!

A few weeks after returning to Hawaii, Cook's crew had once again restocked its supplies and set sail north out of Kealakekua Bay for Maui. But the ships ran into a storm off the coast of the big island, and the *Resolution* suffered a broken foremast. Cook decided to return to Kealakekua Bay to repair the mast. It proved to be a fatal mistake.

TRAGEDY IN PARADISE

When Cook's ship entered the bay on February 11, the islanders were amazed to see him. According to legend, Lono was not expected to reappear for many years. When the natives spotted the broken mast, they began to express doubts about Cook's being their all-powerful, long-awaited savior.

Soon, several of the boldest natives canoed out to Cook's ships and began scavenging for metal objects. Cook warned the Hawaiians to stay away, but to no avail. Finally, Cook could stand no more. He and a party of eleven soldiers set off to the main village to capture the high chief, Kalaniopuu, to hold for ransom until the natives returned the ships' parts. In the meantime, the ships had blockaded the harbor to prevent the Hawaiians from escaping to the neighboring islands by sea. When one Hawaiian canoe attempted to sneak past the blockade, Cook's men opened fire with their muskets, killing several natives, including a lesser chief named Noekema.

Meanwhile, Cook and his men had reached Kalaniopuu's home, and the chief agreed to accompany Cook peacefully. But when the villagers learned that Cook's men had killed Noekema, the Hawaiians suddenly turned on Cook's party. Cook fired his pistol at one of the villagers. In return, the

Hawaiians began throwing stones. Cook's men fired more shots. Before they could reload their muskets, Cook was struck on the head by a large rock. He staggered into the water, where he was stabbed to death by a swarm of angry natives.

When Cook's crew learned of their captain's fate, they went on a rampage, burning the village and killing many Hawaiians. Eventually, Kalaniopuu signed a truce, and Cook's remains were returned to his crew, who buried their captain at sea in a full military funeral.

Cook's crew—saddened at the loss of their great leader—left the islands that March. But Cook's death was not the only tragedy of the voyage. The Hawaiians had managed to turn the iron that the English had left behind into weapons that would eventually change the peace-loving people into savage warriors who would fight among themselves for centuries to come. Worse, still, the diseases that the English explorers had brought to the Hawaiians—diseases to which the natives had no natural immunity—would eventually ravage the Hawaiians, driving them nearly to the point of extinction.

In time, other English explorers began using the maps and drawings that Cook's crew had brought back with them to England. Among the most famous of these explorers was Captain George Vancouver, who brought the first cattle and horses to the islands, and William Bligh, who was captain of the *H.M.S. Bounty* until his crew mutinied and abandoned him and his officers in the South Pacific.

KAMEHAMEHA RULES HAWAII

By the mid-1700s, the Hawaiians had split into four separate warring kingdoms. Less than a decade later, Kamehameha the Great, who would eventually become the first ruler to unite all of the islands, became the sole chief of the big island of Hawaii.

*(opposite page)
This statue at the
Iolani Palace in
Honolulu pays
homage to King
Kamehameha the
Great, the first
ruler to unite the
Hawaiian islands.*

In 1795, after conquering the nearby islands of Maui and Molokai, Kamehameha successfully invaded the island of Oahu in the bloody battle of Nuuanu.

Following these successes, Kamehameha made two attempts to invade the island of Kauai. In 1796 his war canoes were caught in a typhoon and forced to turn back before reaching their destination. In 1804, Kamehameha once again

48

prepared for an attack on Kauai, but his warriors were struck by a feverish disease—most probably cholera contracted from visiting Europeans. His invasion plans were scrapped. But Kamehameha's power was too great for the rulers of Kauai to ignore. In 1810 the Hawaiians of Kauai agreed to sign a treaty accepting the rule of Kamehameha.

By the early 1800s, Hawaii's chiefs had discovered a major new source of wealth. Hawaii was overrun by thick forests of sandalwood, which was popularly used in China as incense. Before long, a profitable three-way trade developed. Americans visiting the islands traded weapons and ammunition for Hawaiian sandalwood. Then they sailed to China, where they traded their cargo of wood for Chinese silk and porcelain, which they carried back to New England to sell at a high profit.

When Kamehameha died in 1819, his son, Liholiho, was named Kamehameha II and took over as ruler of the islands. The new ruler increased the sandalwood harvest by forcing commoners high into the mountains to cut and haul the wood. It was not unusual for workers to carry heavy loads of sandalwood twenty miles or more from the upland forests to ships waiting on the coast. Missionaries who came to the area to spread the word of Christianity reported seeing as many as three thousand men carting wood during the height of the sandalwood trade. By the late 1820s, Hawaii had destroyed most of its sandalwood forests.

A CHANGING WORLD

Throughout the 1820s, a large number of New England Christian missionaries settled in Hawaii. These missionaries helped the Hawaiians establish their first written alphabet so that they could translate and read the Bible. They also established the first American high school west of the Rocky Mountains. Before long, the Hawaiians had taken on Western ways and adopted Western clothing and laws.

In early 1823, Kamehameha II and his queen decided to travel to Europe to visit London. During their stay, the royal couple contracted measles, to which they had no immunity, and died within a few weeks of each other. The ruler's ten-year-old brother was crowned king and named Kamehameha III.

In 1839, Kamehameha III adopted the Declaration of Rights. These laws were soon followed by a written constitution similar to that of the United States. The constitution provided for representative government and two houses of legislature. For the first time in history, popular elections were held in the islands.

By the early 1840s, whaling had replaced all other activities as Hawaii's main source of income. Hawaii was ideally located to become the whaling center of the world—midway between the fertile Arctic and Japanese whaling grounds. At its peak, nearly six hundred whaling ships called on Hawaiian ports each year.

As whaling continued to grow in importance, Hawaii's economy boomed. Hawaiian farmers sold potatoes to supply the ships' crews. Cattle ranches sprang up to furnish the crews with beef. Many Hawaiians themselves joined the whaling crews.

Kamehameha III died in December 1854, and the king's nephew, Alexander Liholiho, was named King Kamehameha IV at the age of twenty-one. But Alexander was destined to a short reign. He died at the age of twenty-nine, and his brother, Lot, was named Kamehameha V.

By 1859 whaling had all but died out as a Hawaiian industry. With the discovery of petroleum products in the United States, there was little demand for whales, from which oil was derived. During the early 1860s, Kamehameha V began promoting the growth of sugar plantations. Hawaii's mild year-round climate proved ideal for the growth of sugarcane, for which American traders were willing to pay dearly.

By this time, the Hawaiian native population had dropped from an estimated several hundred thousand in 1700 to only 70,000 as a result of the continuing spread of diseases brought by visiting foreigners. Seventy thousand natives weren't nearly enough to work the sprawling sugarcane fields. So Kamehameha V established the Bureau of Immigration to encourage people from other lands to immigrate to Hawaii to work on the plantations. Before long, immigrants from China, Japan, Portugal, and Europe began arriving in large numbers. These people eventually intermarried with the Hawaiians, resulting in the great multiracial makeup of the islanders today.

In late 1872, Kamehameha V—the last of the royal Hawaiian line—died without leaving an heir or naming a successor to the throne. For more than two decades, the Hawaiians were torn by political strife as those who favored reinstating the monarchy battled those who preferred constitutional government. The constitutional movement included American businessmen who favored annexing the kingdom for economic reasons.

The constitutional movement finally won with the forced removal from power of Queen Liliuokalani on January 17, 1893, in a revolution led by American businessmen. The Republic of Hawaii was formed the following year.

The U.S. Senate passed a resolution annexing the islands on July 6, 1898, and the United States formally declared Hawaii a U.S. territory on June 14, 1900. Shortly thereafter, new restrictions were placed on the number of Chinese allowed into the islands. To meet the islands' continuing labor shortage, plantation owners began turning to Puerto Rico and Korea for workers. The Filipinos were the last group of immigrants imported to work the island fields. The first major wave arrived in 1906.[1]

Although Chinese, Japanese, Portuguese, Puerto Rican, Korean, and Filipino workers made up the majority of the new Hawaiian immigrants, other field hands came from the South Sea islands, Scotland, Scandinavia, Germany, Great Britain, Spain, and Russia. Each group brought with it its own cultures, foods, and religions. A dozen different languages filled the air in the streets of Honolulu.

During the early 1900s, pineapple farming became Hawaii's second most important industry. American businessman James Dole purchased the island of Lanai in 1922 and turned it into the world's largest pineapple plantation.

Hawaii's first delegate to the U.S. Congress, Prince Jonah Kuhio Kalanianaole, introduced the first bill asking Congress to admit Hawaii as a state in 1919. The bill was defeated. Finally, in 1959, Congress passed legislation making Hawaii a state. On June 27, more than ninety percent of all islanders voted for statehood. On August 21, 1959, after fifty-nine years of territorial status, Hawaii became the nation's 50th state.

CHAPTER SIX

THE GROWTH OF THE SOUTHWEST

By the late 1800s, the southwestern United States was beginning to take shape. California and Nevada were eventually joined in statehood by Colorado (1876), Utah (1896), New Mexico (1912), and Arizona (1912). Hawaii did not enter the Union until 1959, primarily because Congress was hesitant to take in a state with so great a multiracial makeup.

By the mid-1930s, strip mining, which removes large areas of soil to expose coal and other valuable ores, was becoming popular throughout the continental Southwest. Coal, copper, silver, gold, uranium, and other valuable ores began flowing from the strip mines of Arizona, Colorado, New Mexico, Nevada, Utah, and—to a lesser extent—California.

Although strip mines proved to be safer, easier, and more profitable to operate than deep underground mines, they also proved to be harmful to the environment, polluting the air, land, and water. As a result, strip mines have come under pressure from environmentalists who insist that strip mining in the delicate environment of the Southwest should either be made less polluting or be banned altogether—something few southwesterners earning a living from strip mining favor.

By the early 1960s, the traditional industries of mining and ranching were being challenged throughout much of the Southwest by a new source of state and regional income—tourism. Dude ranches, ancient Indian ruins, Old Western towns, and magnificent natural wonders began drawing hundreds of thousands of visitors a year. Large downhill ski resorts in New Mexico, Colorado, Utah, and California attracted millions of additional visitors—all eager to experience the

deep snows and magnificent views from the region's several major mountain ranges.

Meanwhile, southern California and Hawaii began luring tourists eager to sample the states' legendary fishing waters, rich in tuna, wahoo, shark, and other sport fish. Hundreds of thousands more each year came for the sun, scenery, and water sports, such as boating, swimming, and surfing. Thousands more flocked to southern California to tour the giant Hollywood movie studios or take in the wonders of Disneyland, the world's first theme park.

THE SOUTHWEST TODAY

Although the Southwest has changed considerably during the last two decades, the changes have come slowly. Throughout the six-state continental region, mining, ranching, and tourism continue to play an important role in the region's development, while commercial fishing is a valuable industry in both Hawaii and California. U.S. military installations in these two states also provide important strategic defense sites, as well as additional sources of state revenues.

While the region lacks the urban development so common to the central and eastern United States, the Southwest *does* claim four of the twelve largest cities in the nation—Los Angeles and San Francisco in California, Denver in Colorado, and Phoenix in Arizona. Several major industries such as U.S. West, TransAmerica Corp., Chevron, Bank America Corp., Martin Marietta, Wells Fargo, and Continental Airlines provide employment for tens of thousands of southwesterners and products and services to millions of people throughout America and the world.

But perhaps the greatest advantage the Southwest has to offer the world is what it has the most of—clear, sunny skies; warm days and cool nights; and wide open spaces. Even for the three million-plus urbanites living and working in Los Angeles, the Old Southwest is less than half an hour's drive from city limits. There the coyotes still howl at the moon, the cactus stretch toward the midday sky, and the mountains stand guard over the sprawling valleys below.

*(opposite page)
This is a view
from Steamboat
Springs, a small
town nestled into
Colorado's Rocky
Mountains.*

The pioneer spirit that originally forced the Old Southwest open to settlement lives on here, too. Prospectors still search for a big strike among the mountains and streams. Ranchers graze their cattle on land that seems to roll on forever. And fishermen head to sea in search of bountiful harvests.

Things have changed since those first hardy pioneers ventured west in search of new land, new adventure, and a better way of life. But visitors to the Southwest today are still awed by the same challenges that met the early pioneers—the towering mountains, virgin forests, and sprawling deserts. They are what make the Southwest special, different by far from the rest of the United States. They are both its heritage and its future.

A P P E N D I X

STATE FIRSTS

ARIZONA   Statehood: 1912

Franciscan Friar Marcos de Niza became the first Spanish explorer to visit present-day Arizona in 1539. As a result, the area was ruled as part of New Spain from 1598 to 1821.

The first missions were established among the Hopi Indians by 1675, and the first permanent European settlement was founded at Tubac in 1752.

The Roosevelt Dam—the first in Arizona—was completed on the Salt River in 1911, one year before Arizona was admitted to the Union as the nation's 48th state.

CALIFORNIA   Statehood: 1850

Father Junípero Serra, a Franciscan priest, founded the first of a chain of twenty-one Spanish missions in 1769.

A small group of Americans raised the Bear Flag of California at Sonoma on June 14, 1846, proclaiming California an independent republic. They later withdrew their claims after learning that the United States was involved in the Mexican War.

An American prospector, James Marshall, discovered gold in the American River at Sutter's Mill, leading to the famous gold rush of 1849.

The building of the Central Pacific Railroad began in Sacramento and worked its way east across the Sierra Nevada Mountains in 1863.

The first trainload of California oranges left Los Angeles for eastern markets on February 14, 1886.

COLORADO   Statehood: 1876

Zebulon M. Pike became the first white explorer to reach the headwaters of the Arkansas River and discover the mountain peak named in his honor. The first successful ascent of the peak occurrred in 1820 by members of Stephen H. Long's expedition.

Gold was discovered at Cripple Creek in 1891 by Robert Womack, a cowboy.

The first court for the trial of cases involving children was set up in Denver in 1899 under the guidance of Judge Benjamin B. Lindsey. The court subsequently served as a pattern for similar courts throughout the world.

HAWAII   Statehood: 1959

The first Polynesians arrived in Hawaii between A.D. 300 and 500; other groups arrived in the 900s and 1200s.

Captain James Cook became the first European to visit the islands in 1778. He was killed by irate islanders one year later.

NEVADA   Statehood: 1864

The state's first major gold strike, the Comstock Lode, was made at Virginia City in 1859, attracting miners from around the world. Other strikes followed at Hamilton, Gold Hill, Eureka, and Austin.

NEW MEXICO   Statehood: 1912

The nation's oldest government building, the Palace of the Governors, was erected at Santa Fe in 1610. Officials of Spain and, later, Mexico used the building to administer the province for more than two centuries.

In 1800, Mexican miners discovered huge deposits of copper ore at Santa Rita, near Silver City.

William Becknell brought the first wagonloads of goods from Missouri across the Santa Fe Trail in 1822. Other traders, lured by the high prices New Mexicans were willing to pay for manufactured goods and the low price of furs, soon followed. Regular stagecoach service was established between Santa Fe and Independence, Missouri, in 1849.

Carlsbad Caverns, one of the world's great natural wonders, were discovered in 1901 by Jim White, a cowboy, after he spied a large flock of bats emerging from an opening in the ground at dusk.

UTAH   Statehood: 1896

In 1824 famed trapper and scout Jim Bridger discovered the Great Salt Lake, one part of a giant inland sea. With Kit Carson as his guide, John Frémont explored the Great Basin in 1843.

At Promontory Point on May 10, 1869, a Central Pacific train from Sacramento met a Union Pacific train from Omaha, marking the beginning of the first transcontinental railroad. The final spike, made of gold, was driven by California governor Leland Stanford.

NOTES

CHAPTER TWO
A CLASH OF CULTURES

1. Carl Ubbelohde, Maxine Benson, and Duane A. Smith, *A Colorado History* (Boulder, Colo.: Pruett Publishing Company, 1988), p. 32.

CHAPTER THREE
EAST MEETS WEST

1. George Brown Tindall, *America: A Narrative History* (New York: W. W. Norton & Company, 1984), p. 473.
2. Alvin M. Josephy, Jr., *The Civil War in the American West* (New York: Alfred A. Knopf, 1991), p. 80.
3. Ibid, pp. 81–85.
4. Donald Dale Jackson, "Sojourners Who Came to Stay" (*Smithsonian*, February 1991), p. 116.

CHAPTER FOUR
LIFE ON THE RANGE

1. Ubbelohde, Benson, and Smith, *A Colorado History*, pp. 113–114.
2. Tindall, *America: A Narrative History*, p. 731.
3. Herbert J. Bass, *People in Time and Place* (Morristown, N.J.: Silver Burdett & Ginn, 1991), pp. 480–481.

CHAPTER FIVE
WEST TO HAWAII

1. Glenda Bendure and Ned Friary, *Hawaii* (Hawthorne, Vic 3122, Australia: Lonely Planet Publications, 1990), p. 21.

SELECTED BIBLIOGRAPHY

Bass, Herbert J. *People in Time and Place*. Morristown, N.J.: Silver Burdett & Ginn, 1991.

Dillon, Richard H. *North American Indian Wars*. New York: Facts on File, 1983.

Gutman, Herbert G. *Who Built America?* New York: Pantheon Books, 1989.

Josephy, Jr., Alvin M. *The Civil War in the American West*. New York: Alfred A. Knopf, 1991.

Tindall, George Brown. *America: A Narrative History*. New York: W. W. Norton & Company, 1984.

Ubbelohde, Carl, Maxine Benson, and Duane A. Smith. *A Colorado History*. Boulder, Colo.: Pruett Publishing Company, 1988.

Wissler, Clark. *Indians of the United States*. New York: Anchor Books, 1989.

Wright, John W., ed. *The Universal Almanac*. Kansas City: Universal Press Syndicate, 1990.

SUGGESTED READING

The American Way West. New York: Facts on File, 1990.

Aylesworth, Thomas G., and Virginia L. Aylesworth. *The Southwest*. New York: Chelsea House, 1992.

Behrens, June. *A New Flag for a New Country*. Chicago: Childrens Press, 1975.

Billington, Ray Allen. *Westward Expansion: A History of the American Frontier*. New York: Macmillan Publishing Co., Inc., 1974.

Dillon, Richard H. *North American Indian Wars*. New York: Facts on File, 1983.

Freedman, Russell. *Indian Chiefs*. New York: Holiday House, 1987.

Smith, Carter. *A Sourcebook on the American West: Exploring the Frontier*. Brookfield, Conn.: The Millbrook Press, 1992.

———. *A Sourcebook on the American West: Native Americans of the West*. Brookfield, Conn.: The Millbrook Press, 1992.

INDEX

3